4 Rms w Vu

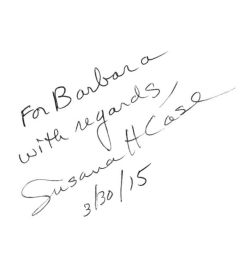

4 Rms w Vu

Poems by Susana H. Case

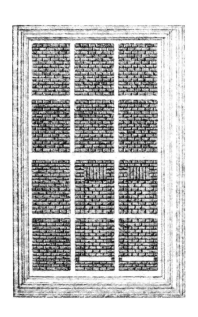

Mayapple Press 2014

Published by   MAYAPPLE PRESS
                362 Chestnut Hill Rd.
                Woodstock, NY 12498
                www.mayapplepress.com

ISBN 978-1-936419-39-5
Library of Congress Control Number: 2014935312

ACKNOWLEDGMENTS

Grateful acknowledgment is made to the following where these poems have previously appeared, sometimes in different form:

88: A Journal of Contemporary American Poetry: Picture Rocks Wash; *Amoskeag:* Limited Sight Distance; *Bayou Magazine:* Apartment House, New York City, 1 A.M. (as Apartment House, 1 A.M.); *BigCityLit:* Socks; *Bluestem:* Bamboo Room, Carve; *Borderlands: Texas Poetry Review:* Coyote City; *Bridges:* In Hospital; *Cider Press Review:* Incantation, San-jûrô, as Played by Toshirô Mifune, Occupies the Body of a Yard Guy; *Coe Review:* Why the Dreamer Misjudges; *The Dos Passos Review:* And Now Let's Consider Sex and Death; *Earth's Daughters:* Year of Our Lost Dog; *Eclipse:* Ephemera, *Mr. Verner asks New York not to spoil his friend, the Bushman; The Evening Street Review:* Transformational Grammar; *Front Range:* Annette Funicello Eyes; *Gin Bender Poetry Review:* The Lasting of It; *Gulf Stream Magazine:* A Touch of Mink; *Hawai'i Pacific Review:* As If the Sand Were Stone, Space Contracts What It Contains; *Iron Horse Literary Review:* Still Life with Frogs in Fog; *Mochila Review:* Allegory of Brutality, Little Neanderthal; *Newtown Literary:* Omega; *Northwind:* Disappearing Act; *Oyez Review:* Springing Abbie Hoffman from Jail; *Pebble Lake Review:* A Diagonal Break; *Picayune:* That Adirondack Summer with You; *Poetry South:* Three Thousand Days of Evil Tongues; *Portland Review:* Adobe Baby—, Dark Matter; *Potomac Review:* Action at a Distance; *San Pedro River Review:* Bring Me the Baroque; *Saranac Review:* Barn Rolling Downhill; *Slant:* After the Last Inca Ruler, Talk About Consciousness; *Stone Highway Review:* Night Noir; *Valley Voices: A Literary Review:* Another Poem About a Train Ride; *Visions-International:* Generation; *Xanadu:* Interior.

Some poems have previously appeared in the chapbooks: *Anthropologist in Ohio*, Main Street Rag Publishing Company, *The Cost of Heat*, Pecan Grove Press, and *Manual of Practical Sexual Advice*, Kattywompus Press, and in the anthologies: Margot Wizansky, ed. *Rough Places Plain: Poems of the Mountains*, Salt Marsh Pottery Press and Gerry LaFemina, ed. *Token Entry: New York City Subway Poems*, Smalls Books.

Cover photo by Susana H. Case. Cover designed by Judith Kerman. Interior artwork by Eric A. Hoffmann. Book designed and typeset by Amee Schmidt with titles in Franklin Gothic Medium and text in Georgia. Author photo courtesy of Ricardo Andre.

Contents

1. Bedroom—
For the Second Husband

2. Family Room—
For the Children, the Parents

3. Storage Room—
For the First Husband, the Lovers

4. Dying Room—
For the Gone, the Diminished

For Ben (d. 1994) and Sophie Zura Case (d. 1993)

1. Bedroom—
For the Second Husband

My hands
invent another body for your body

        —Octavio Paz

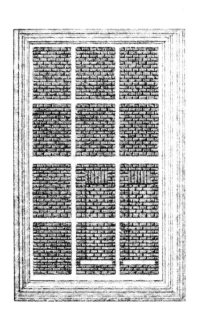

Dark Matter

Anyway, I have no idea why I fall in love
with you. It's sleep deprivation,
dinners at 4 a.m. in the emptying 24-hour
coffee shop on 3rd Street, the ketchup

darkening the rim of the bottle, the table sticky
with grease, Merle Haggard on the next booth's
jukebox, hookers eating meatloaf. All this time,
you're too skinny even for me, angle and bone,

smoking away the night, honing your art persona.
I'm always hungry
until it gets too hot and then
I'm never hungry.

What happens when neither of us works
a regular job—we fight
the slick of moisture that spells summer,
my cheap air conditioner that doesn't blow

hard enough, the grime in my sheets
we hardly ever get around to changing.
We fight a foreign war.
We fight each other,

stab at the core of domesticity and watch
it seep. We even find a dog.
The mystery of what will happen next,
like the Large Hadron Collider

nested between Switzerland and France,
potential micro black holes and strangelets
that can swallow us—these hours,
the closest we will ever be to God.

Adobe Baby—

Be my abode. My foundation
wall. Mud block
and concrete node—press

yourself to me, adore me, dogged
like a proud West Texas
fly. It's all irregular anyway,

the surface, you, lust-laced glue—
Baby, drive out past the tourist viewpoint
for the hokey Marfa lights tonight,

beat close encounters
with the flash of inexplicable. Leave
lodestar, antelope, commitment

phobia along the pavement edge
of geometric envelope. In moments
we can do the tra la la,

lob lies, be *Only You*,
inextricable knot of limbs. Forget
corrosion caused by time—it's turbinate

love: (1) bodies in electric glide
(2) trajectory written in unpacked code
—um? um? huh?

(3) surely soon to be boulder
slide. Why not? It seems to never
happen for me any other way.

Year of Our Lost Dog

Blame
becomes a broken object,
a game, another thing to be mended,
except, the dog was found.
(She stuck to the chase of a rodent off a trail,
slipped onto a ledge.) It's the year
of our lost dog anyway—my fault, my tenacity
—your fault

for our momentary distraction, your fear
of height on a rocky incline,
the fault line of guilt.
Up to the top and back, I walked in tears
calling her name. I planned
to stay and search all new-moon
night, pictured coyotes ripping
the softness of her belly, the slick
of viscera. I could smell,
I thought, her fear and mine.

Under the quilt, at night, night
after night, dog at the headboard
snoring, I trace the clenching
in my groin and brain when I round
another curve of reverie, and still,
no dog appears. I can't let go
of the presence of absence,
reach to pet her head.

You stayed back that day to root around
in the off-trail undergrowth,
the crunch of leaves under your boots,
heard the faint *tin tin*
of her collar tags. Looking shakily out
from a cliff, you found her a short way down,
scared silent. Five minutes
after her rescue, she didn't remember.
Always like that, I make you
hero and villain.

Action at a Distance

Entangled system of two objects—
you could affect me
halfway across the universe.

Einstein didn't think anyone
could travel that fast.
He didn't know *us*.

Einstein wrote his wife letters—
expect no tenderness
—his mathematical donkey,

goitered, limping, bookish.
I absorb your gauge
bosons. We are bound together.

Observe one of the pair,
know the other.
Tenderness. One stone. *Ein stein.*

All marriages are dangerous.
His was sad, fateful,
Einstein riding a beam of light.

The Red Lighter

To help me ignore the electrical waves
raucous and unruly
that violate the cave of my skull,
to help me relax,
you buy me packs of cigarettes
and a flash-red lighter that screams sex
louder than it screams illness or death.
Your plan works.

Sensual stroke and metal click
mark the pleasure
from things really good at what they do.
The coating matches
my saturated lips,
my nails.
There's something about it—a wheelbarrow
can't hold a candle to it.

I haven't smoked in twenty years
—think of mortality
and relearn pacing.
The mountain of ash in the ashtray
marks the slippage of bad days.
On the better days
I am a tarted-up Monica Vitti
and suddenly my hair is blond.

It's my Döbereiner's Lamp,
my catalyst,
the seductive monster-thing
like you
loved by women sharp and loose.
Insouciant flame,
no blame.
So good when you put your hand on mine
—then light it for me.

Three Thousand Days of Evil Tongues

On the steps of the white limestone
Mosteiro Dos Jerónimos in Belem, away

from the talk of presumed friends, I pose
for you. My tight smile bruises the air.

Bundled in a fringed shawl wrapped
around a thin black leather jacket—

I bought them to look hip—I try not to squint.
If I were not your wife, would you choose me now?

Hazy, hard to see
the digital photo we debate saving,

we resist the glare in a shadowed entrance,
the south one with coral and sea shells.

Inside, built from pepper, are the Manueline cloisters,
profits of the spice trade, where Luís de Camões

is buried. He was targeted with gossip
for a love affair, described his stay in Lisbon

as three thousand days of evil tongues.
Fresh calla lilies apron his tomb.

*If there had been more of the world, they would
have reached it.* Would *we*?

What else is there to say? If I were not your wife,
would you choose me now?

Space Contracts What It Contains

I wonder if the root-bound
palm is ecstatic in its pot,
or squirms in non-
repose. On our cramp
of a couch—you, me—
domestic, a portrait
like an Edouard Vuillard,
yellow-flowered wallpaper. We lean
against each other
in this room of diminished
air. Cracking lead-based
paint for trim, dingy rough-
sewn lampshade
show their age
like me. Here's a confession:
I'm distempered
for no reason—I feel
like being alone. You close
your eyes and snore. Too tight,
the space contains us,
including me in clinging jeans.
Our dear dead dog, ashes
in a blue nightstand box,
compacts down to bone.

Bring Me the Baroque

Not just babbled love
—steal it if you have to—I want
the concrete evidence, before life cracks
apart, yes, the gold Oaxacan earrings,
Sicilian rustications on the stonework
of my palazzo,
but also the smear of dark
red lipstick on my pillow.
Bring me patchouli oil
to rub on my sheets and don't forget
the transcendent knowledge
I lack; I want to know if faith's validated
and before the viscera rot, don't neglect
the food—bring me something good
—you cook the best
squid in tomato sauce and let me scream
until I'm hoarse how
fine it feels when you get down
on your knees on the bedroom
floor and paint my toes, that same red
that's in our lip-smeared bed, that music
in my head.
So bring me all of it,
chained to my dreams until you're weary
with the load; when we're old and the earth
breaks up, we'll drag
the rubble with us, in a tumbrel.

Touch of Mink

When a prosperous Cary Grant flies
an unemployed Doris Day
to Bermuda, a Hollywood Bermuda
framed in the window of their coral
block cottage—not a real cottage,
but a movie cottage
that would never gray with mold
in sixty-eight percent
humidity—the light
that massed clouds and moistness
filter into emeralds is more rarified
than in the real Bermuda;
it never rains,
not at 2 a.m. on TV,
which we watch when we can't sleep.

And when Cary Grant
in his beautiful suit says,
*I pretended to be somebody I wanted to be
until finally I became that person,*
we acknowledge we want
to be that person, too,
especially in Cary Grant's Bermuda where
there's no graying of hair and even
cheap Chardonnay tastes French.

Sure, some critics call this life
a *featherweight farce*, but we know
no Doris Day would ever refuse
Cary Grant in his Bermuda.
Nor would we give back a paid-for
Norell designer wardrobe, including mink
despite not needing it in the heat.

And never mind the heat
in that Bermuda or the need
to go swimming in Church Bay

with parrotfish, their dark
stripes, dots, and crayon
colors, to cool off—
we're always cool;
we're always on the ball

and if there's any anxiety
about our sexual selves or romance,
it's only that it's written into the script.

And Now Let's Revisit Sex and Death

Getting into bed with you,
it's afternoon, my mind on play,
I'm wearing chiffon, I'm grinning
like the cows have already come home
for me when you say,
could you take a look at my lip—I'm thinking cancer,
which of course stops the whole thing dead
while we go to the lamp,
get you angled right and yes,
there's something there, could be anything,
there's a definite *thing* that doesn't belong,
like a dog in a tree
and you couldn't know the number of my women friends
whose men are no longer here,
how it always starts with,
could you look at this bump on my neck, this spot on my leg,
as if any of us had expertise in more than fear and rage,
rage because you just had to wrap your lips
around your smoke, didn't you, instead of around
some more compliant part of me,
always this conjunction of sex and death,
it's like the good twin hopelessly
sharing a brain with the evil twin,
the one who pops open a beer,
whispers, *go ahead—light the match—mess it all up*,
through nicotine-yellow teeth, the one
who makes me think that if you're ill,
I'll shoot you myself, kill you right now
for carelessly leaving me in this fucked-up place alone.

Socks

Standing over opposite sides of the bed
as if it were a boxing ring,
which it is not, most of the time,

we sort socks: black argyle
socks, red purple ruffled French
socks, fish-net sex socks. I must

toss the ones unpaired
or with holes for toes, persistent toes
that feel like icicles curled against mine,

an encircling. If tonight is quiet
enough in my head, I shall hear both
our dogs wheezing; I shall hear our clocks

chime. I shall hear your breathing.
No sleep. Instead, I count each scratch
of your toenails against my legs

because you forgot to file them down again,
the accidental elbow in the face
in a too-small bed. Also, the number

of times you touched me gently that day
in all the so-sweet places. No sleep,
as I wonder who will break

the circle first. And if you do
—because so often the men go first—
what I shall write of you when you are gone.

2. Family Room—
For the Children, the Parents

her memories falling back,
her life welcoming her where she belongs.

—Virgil Suarez

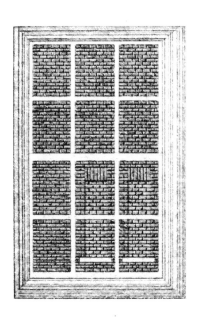

Generation

Father wanted a boy, wrote a letter
to my unborn son...
Instead I came out—soft, pink,
loud. He got used to it.
There the line, fettered, stopped—
their only child, no real companion.
I got used to it.

Cleaning out their home, I rescue
an old photo album: stiffened
by the aperture, grandfather
in a heavy brown woolen suit,
glitter of his new gold watch chain
stored now in my bedroom
drawer, grandmother's hair pulled
back with tortoise combs
brought in a single suitcase from Kiev.
They hardly knew one another.
I hardly knew them. In another photo,
mother tries to smile, her dark marcelled
hair. And there I am, twenty-three, in beat
black jeans. Hands draping
skinny hips, I lean back against
the safety of a red brick wall, frowning.

Where are *you*? Why
am I slogging through fog, alone? You won't
amble by, fill the space
for another decade. You won't want a child.
I'll want you so much, I'll get used to it.

I look out at air, at
my father behind the lens, so expectant.

Transformational Grammar

My English teacher father
drilled me to diagram sentences
with Reed-Kellogg trees.
The branches were dry
as my mother's hamburgers.
I preferred shoplifting lipsticks to parsing,
sex with boys in cars,
my lips smeared with *Sheer Iced Raisin,*
wet from peach jug wine.

My father liked Gertrude Stein's comment
that nothing *has ever been more exciting*
than diagramming sentences.
He liked the beauty of clarity,
the fit of abstract parts—
balloon architecture,
a staircase of gerunds.
I was chaos, the late-life wild child.
I didn't know how to be subordinate,
alive to my power to wound.

He threatened my boyfriend: *come near*
my daughter again, I'll castrate you.
We rode off, laughing, Corvair
radio blasting Darlene Love,
our own girl group wall of sound.
Next day, on the way to work,
my father crashed his Buick
into a parked car, cracked his ribs.
That was it for his Buick.

Little Neanderthal

Scladina DNA—from a Belgian cave,
Meuse Basin divergence,
a molar found, grooved

enamel from scarcity of food, the size
of an incisor from my old dog,
saved in a box. I miss her,

my heavy-browed stocky dog.
I don't know if *this* heavy-browed
toothy child could speak,

or was the first autist,
if this child craved
delicate shell necklaces,

bone pendants, crushed
by now in earth, a wing bone flute
for playing diatonic scales

over a father's grave:
do re mi.... Me, my
own mouth, its wobbly molar.

A child gazes
across tundra at ibex, bison
—needs a new rawhide coat.

Elongated blades, chert scrapers
strip the animal skin before
the fading away of a people.

Andean Indians, the Aymara,
say the past
lies ahead of you

—*front time*.
Behind you
is the future. True unknown.

Annette Funicello Eyes

Technician with electric pen,
needles at the end, tattoos
black eyeliner onto my lids.
Make it dramatic, I say—no natural look.
Eyebrows inked into a perfect arch;
she takes a ruler, checks
the geometry of her work.
Who said beauty was painless?
Not this new me, perky
Beach Blanket Bingo dark-eyed 1960s
Annette Funicello me.

Six thousand letters
of love Annette got, every
virginal Mouseketeer month—
her breasts poking out like Mount Etna
and Mount Vesuvius earlier than
on the rest of us. My friend Lizzie's father
had a crush on her, cried
at the rumor she'd died (she hadn't).
I studied this—was seven,
had never seen a grown man weep.

Why the Dreamer Misjudges

The pediatrician told my parents
that an oozy vagina
meant I was oversexed, advised

them to inspect
my underwear, drug me through my teens with
aqua-black tranquilizing pills

that didn't work.
At fifteen, my period wouldn't start, then
wouldn't stop

and the new gynecologist—I wouldn't
go back to the baby doctor—said to keep me
home from school with an icepack

between my bloody thighs, during which time
I read Freud's
The Interpretation Of Dreams. Each night's dream,

a huge rusting industrial beast
would penetrate me, the only human in that place,
but I was blind and in the middle of experiencing

one of the *three great humiliations in human history,*
the discovery that I wasn't in control
of my body—or mind.

Disappearing Act

A thin, blond woman with a leash
walks a dwarf rabbit
in the old part of Lucca.
She is proud,
holds up her pet to stroke. The creature
likes the fresh grass in the park,
shakes at my touch.
I can't resist the softness,
the almost-cleft lip.

Teenagers come to smoke.
Without two pennies to rub together,
they rub together—that respite
before adult life. What I knew then,
without knowing: in first high heels,
rummaging in recklessness,
I flowed into every boy who offered.

For four days, I return each afternoon
after photographing walls—time-worn
bricks, their surprising vulnerabilities.
The park bench is good for smoking.
The same girl sits on the boy,
confidently daring him.
The woman and her rabbit—
I don't see them again.

Limited Sight Distance

Howie, already wasted on smack
when the Friday night school dance
began, sat on the curb singing

off key with the oldies—Shep and the Heartbeats,
A Thousand Miles Away.
We were too hip to break a sweat, though

white kids—one notch down.
It's no fun, waking up
next to garbage cans, Howie said

as I ran fingers though his surfer-dyed hair.
I'd never awakened anywhere except my own
sweet ruffled bed. The world,

a wide open bottle of pills—at thirteen,
that's what I knew. And I knew every
group, every label of the music that came out

from that packed gym.
I had cool shades on. Rhinestones
on the ends sparkled under street-light.

Laura on the roof, five months pregnant
—she just that day found out—
worked up the nerve to toss herself off.

In the Institution

They say she killed her baby—
what do they know of her life,
she asks the bored
attendant in the pale green
recreation room where she gnaws at
the circumstances of her incarceration,
transubstantiation of real life, this dream
as crazy Madonna with dead child.
The blue form that silently blurted out
onto the cold tile
of her parents' bathroom floor,
a complication among yellow towels.
She cut the cord.
There would be no name.

What did they know,
so small their view?
So small, the on-off switch,
the towel on the mouth, the stilling.
And if it had been stillborn,
how that would have changed
her life, razor pressed against wrist—
her bandaged wrist.

Once a Bunsen burner, her will
is stilled by cups of pills. She wants
out. She carries in her head
the idea of the child
more real than her own life. Tired
of gray linoleum, overly-bright jello,
she is afraid that outside
the sky is the same blue as before.

The Lasting of It

Right before the crash,
we sat in my dad's green Chevy
compact—the one he'd gifted us
with the weary engine rings.
You yelled,
I listened to the air conditioner
drone, when that morning's smashup
fractured the arc of fight.
It broke our windshield,
the other car's swerve to avoid
a third car that got away clean.
When I felt the glass
and saw crushed fender
everywhere and that we hadn't
even begun to move,
I realized we hadn't made
any headway in years

—the other couple
screaming about the broken glass
all over the baby seat, the luck
that they'd left him home.
I was childless
and stunned in a persistent way,
relieved that you were finally quiet.

You got a hammer, knelt in the dust,
banged out the fender
until it no longer locked the wheel.
We continued on, soon ended it.
That's most of what I remember now—
a hard smack,
unclean break,
and how we didn't even begin
to escape without a scratch.

In Hospital

The slight feel of your hand on my back
grounds me.

Adamant she didn't want to die,
caught in a net of cables, tubes,
she is already distended, cannot be moved.
White uniforms, floating sharks;
I had thought it would be her heart.

Stranded. Green walls, this silent white.
Better not to swim here, so easy
for them—her clouded-over eye,
watery sick.

I want to take her home.
You will take *me* home.
She will die alone.

And I try not to move,
afraid to bleed.

Girls You Could Love

girls you could fuck
and straddle-both-worlds girls
like me, you showed off

to your friends. Peaking early
girls. Peaking late. Prom queens.
Science girls. Nasty girls.

Straight-A girl with my intricate
knowledge of each protrusion, slit,
crevice. *Don't forget the stockings,*

the heels, you'd say, fetish boy
with your dual-career
parents, your empty house,

housekeeper who pretended
not to notice, the gilt phones I laughed
about to my friends. So good to be

inside you—or—you
inside me. I got so lost in it. My parents
who devoured relationship

books frowned, *symbiosis*
—a big word for us, fat
on the tongue—and yes,

I thought I'd crumple without
you, but also knew to direct you, *slowly
run your hand up here,* along the 15 denier

nylon you had so crazily fixed upon. Little
garter button indents red on my thighs
that read: the one with these legs

knows exactly how to want.
Anyone who thought the power was yours
really didn't understand.

3. Storage Room—
For the First Husband, the Lovers

My noon, my midnight, my talk, my song;
I thought that love would last forever: I was wrong.

—*W. H. Auden*

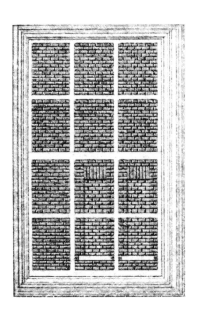

Still Life with Frogs in Fog

We think too small, like the frog
at the bottom of the well.
*   —Mao Tse-Tung*

In most of my memories, you're driving.
Gray damp on our windshield. Traffic,
a lot of it. Accident ahead. One car,
green, mounting another, blue
—the way frogs mate.
Rayne, Louisiana,
Frog Capital of the World.

That summer of love's waning, thousands
of tiny frogs rain
onto Odžaci in Serbia. On the roadside, crushed
clumps of frog, their poisonous skin.

Talk trailing off like touch before it.
The thing about driving,
you face forward. No eye contact,
no 180 degree field of vision.
Which of us decided first
it was better not to look?

The last tow truck pulls out onto the roadbed;
chained blue wreck hangs from its frame.

Absolute and Comparative

You were the best of men.
The worst. What I knew—you,

nurturer of orchids, dogs,
presented me with a red ceramic flower pot,

rolled on the floor, mock-wrestling
with the cow-hocked glossy black puppy

keen to do good. Before you went mad,
an inside bolt nudged loose.

In the mornings you were better,
not yet clocked for conflict:

coffee warming, the sun a cardboard sword,
its sharp stabs through too much glass

muffled by the warp and weft of bathrobes.
What I didn't know—whose hand

ruffed the switch that pulled
the dollhouse down? Better would wither

to worse with the first martini, thin-curled
yellow slice; there were too many.

The clocks in this room now tick
as if all loneliness happens at once.

Carve

Man on the subway train, *carve* on his arm—
quick bluish tattoo letters.
Near Thanksgiving, I'm thinking knife, poultry,
a crowd in rush hour like a barn full
of turkeys, thick with unarticulated words.
More than four and a half million people
ride underground each day in New York,
most without a verb in pigment on bare
skin. He's in leather and jeans—
could probably carve a turkey with his teeth.

My heart carved from alabaster—constant friction
and in a moment everything
unprotected gives way. Starter stone,
starter connection. Fragile stone—cater
to the inherent *bruise* lines of alabaster or
increase the probability of breakage.

To scratch, to write, to cut
with precision. To cut into pieces.
I didn't read the danger.
It's now possible to carve with electricity.
So many times electric, carved
into golden bed sheets.

Relativity of pain—as a child,
I fell on broken glass,
cut my face. Inadvertent tattoo.
In this city, most scarification
is in an instant.

Vibration and sting of needle. Indelible
insertion of ink. I know better now,
made myself a hardened leathery crust.
Man on the train,
injunction on his arm—I've been staring,
contemplating meaning. He smiles benignly.
Must be my newfound intricate *Moko,*
become visible: connoisseur
of irony, guardian lizard god.

Mountain Path

Before the dissection of what went wrong,
we walked wide sand past ocotillo,
cholla, mesquite, narrow gravel
switchbacks to the ridge-line junction
under full moon.
Drunk on carbon monoxide,
the city in the distance sprawled
across the valley floor. Horses
with harness bells moved somewhere below.
You carried most of the water
and most of the sorrows.
I had the camera and was pretty then.
Too many flash photographs
among paloverde, cactus—I thought
they would build memories—when the green
coat of a saguaro just right
in the refraction
could clarify the reason for everything—
all I needed for a perfect life.

Barn Rolling Downhill

Our final car trip, we visit Kansas
early twentieth century round barns—
one built with a Sears Roebuck kit.
Leaky roofs.
Weathervanes pinged from target shoots.
I take photographs—you against rotting sides.

Such frugal shapes, this husbandry
of wood—a farmer once saved
a third to a half of the cost of a rectangle's
materials. The Kansas plain, nothing flatter,
except us, this vacation,
its moan there and then back to the bumpy
foothills of Ohio.

First day home, we sleep in all morning.
Your grizzled face burrows the pillow,
so far from reaching-range, even farther,
it seems, than Kansas.
All our potentiality defies salvation.
Let's just say it's a round barn
rolling downhill, the pebbled world
knocking against the same old staves.

Another Poem About a Train Ride

Last time I came clattering through here
on this train, we were still a couple,
unlikely though it seems now.
We came for cocktails at your boss's
oversized house stuck on the harbor
and stuffed with French provincial,
white and gold-embellished.
This demand for an appearance—
he chose your Rolex, lectured
on what it meant to wear the right suit,
reminded you
what it meant to have a mentor.
You hated him, hated that job more,
but thought we needed it. *You* needed it,
fake bohemian in corporate clothing
carefully building your Rolodex.

The house was noisy, a hundred people.
Back then, one could still smoke
inside. The house was full of smoke.
There was a maid offering sausages
on a tray. *Eat one*, you hissed.
I was a vegetarian, folksinger wannabe.
I wondered if anyone liked the boss,
if even the boss's wife liked the boss,
or if all of it was fear.
It was fear.
Already, at the edges, I had fear of you,
the underling.
I didn't know the ubiquity then
—the one in ten rate for bully bosses,
didn't know the rate for bully husbands.
By the fourth gin martini,
drunk and avuncular—
if you play your cards right, he told us,
you too will live like this.

That Adirondack Summer with You

The first tree frogs make us hysterical—
we're drunk from sparkling wine.
     Call me irresponsible
According to my book,
the hairy woodpeckers are not woodpeckers,
but yellow-bellied sapsuckers.
     Yes, I'm unreliable
A week of firsts in the sticks—the black flies,
we can't lie on the deck to watch the eclipse.
     Throw in undependable
Before the trees close up,
one last view of Oven Mountain.

In July, we are without air conditioning,
melting ice on each other's skin.
     Rainbows, I'm inclined to pursue
And then your lies begin.
     Foolish alibis
Chirping sparrows by the woodshed;
in bed, I put headphones on to block the sound.
     It's undeniably true

By August, most of the bugs have flown the coop.
We hang soap on the slope of the hill
to keep the deer from eating the flowers.
     I'm not too clever, I just adore you
But the leaves begin to die.
The hummingbirds leave.
Ravens eat the last blackberries.

Night Noir

We lie in bed angry and silent—
the hammering outside
a type of bleeding.
Too much exhaustion to look.

Urban brick cliff apartments,
depositories for delusion
and dinner deliveries—
only God makes better pizza
—and a frieze of maids
with swollen ankles.
They're from far away
places with beaches and sun.

Nights like this, children
gather to smoke
rough-rolled joints by the river,
a raucous antidote to futures
dissolved
to flat screens and cubicles,

and the hoarse moan for more
of anything
rivals the hammering
as our lips kiss—
zest into stickiness and sad

nostalgia, sweet-tasting
poison, anti-freeze thickening
in the shaded furrows
of the gutter. Our lips,
their imprecise account
of love, this prison
of waning moon and cervix.

Loneliest Planet

In the movie, an American couple treks
the Caucasus and mostly what I see
are mountains and what I hear
are sounds of shifting pebbles underfoot
and it reminds me of when you and I
used to walk through mountains,
because even before they're not talking,
they're not talking. Then a gunman appears
because these are the Kazakhstan steppes,
and the plot pivots,
man becomes lummox as he shoves
his honey in front of the gun
to protect himself before his better self
resurrects. That's all it takes, the one
mistake that can never be erased,
that reminds me of what we could never erase:
a battened farmhouse,
the Lake District of England,
nothing at night but damp and stars
and the massif of our impasse.
I'm humming *loneliest star from the sun*,
your voice suspended in the quiet
like the sword of Dionysius,
threat always in the parable,
your snarl that if I left you, you'd fight me
for every single dollar—
the words that shatter the spell,

turn everything we had together
to gravel, especially the
fells and crags rising around us.

Picture Rocks Wash

My throat fatigues from the morning's silence
between us. In that time before the dissolution,
one hundred and three degrees,
we look for the hummingbird
nest, wonder if it's true
they build new upon old
—slur of years,
a layer of debris
upon stolen spider webbing.
Last season, she built the nest too low,
sat unprotected.
The straps
of my pack chafe.
I pause in the sand, tighten.
Your back gets small as you hurry
toward the break of rocks, a need
even in this to be first. In my mind,
the well-known contours of your face
already liquid, blurring.

The Weightlessness of Birds

Pleased to be leaving you for a better,
more affordable space, my hallelujah,
afterward, you would say I was happy.
I left my art books behind, even Audubon
and Klee. You helped me carry
two floor lamps up Seventh Avenue,
not enough to light my new apartment
—New York's mean sunlight.

Afterward, of course I was happy,
the lie of initial
intoxication, of breathing.
I need to explain this testimony,
sewing a lavender damask curtain
for the shower, ordering
Moo Shu Pork, relieved
to have survived you.

The box of frozen peas
pressed on bruises, I had adjusted
to the *ex*. For the purple finches
I hung a feeder. In flower boxes
I tried bulbs, purple tulips
on the cracked patio, dahlias
around the edge of the beds.
Nothing ever grew in my new home.

About the weightlessness of birds,
how a thin, banded leg
lifts clear, about the weight
of Charlie Bird Parker's horn, his song,
Ornithology—I thought about them all.
Told my friends now even I felt free.
Once you and I were done, I slept,
my ground floor room's back door
wide open. A woman screamed
lightly in the night, *No! Please! Don't!*
—I telephoned for help, hoped
someone fingerprinting her skin
wouldn't surely be her lover.

Bamboo Room

Auction lots. I want the Asian batik,
bicycle tracks transecting
six peacocks. The curved tan bamboo
couch and chair set. If the price is right,
you whisper. I'm in poker face
with unfaithful eye, don't stare
at any one desired object too long.

Three years later, marriage over,
in my new apartment—an oversized
gaggle of bentwood scolds,
cackling at my willingness to pay too much.
When I cede the set a year later,
it's really over; I'm rid of the reproaching
couch, its looped-arm reminder
of too much time circling backward.

I keep the batik, its brown panels,
nine snakes, the peacock border. In the center,
fish and squat men. I imagine
it set on grass, dipped resist wax
hardening. The artist applies design dye,
waits. A crinkly glint reflected
off micaceous rock seduces
her always wandering attention; she leaves
the fabric unprotected. In this moment,
her husband mounts his bicycle,
begins to ride carelessly away from her,
toward the village edge.

Allegory of Brutality

Marina Abramović,
in a long white dress,
scrubs the meat and gristle
off six thousand pounds
of cow bones
six hours a day
in a hot basement.
We're at the Venice Biennale,
Balkan Baroque,
a mountain of ossein, blood.
Skin rubbed raw, art carcass,
she sings a lament.

You are my mournful song
and, like lovers everywhere,
there's blood on our hands:
damage we do,
weep and stink
of everyday brutality.
Yes, less than that of war,
but within us, the butcher,
the grieving flesh.
Here is water,
soap, lemon—
all impossibility.

Martyrdom

Stone-hard, each tender touch
exposed to air. Your reticence
evokes secrets from Rome's catacombs.
Preserved emotion,
like a Eucharist fresco in San Callisto.
Your chest, its loculus,
a sarcophagus: I want to ransack
your deep-buried treasures.
When I spit out
I love you, I see the perfect
arcosolium framed
by your brow, a scurrying burial
of response. So difficult
to depose the dead, their silent oath,
the weak possibility of resurrection.

The dash of your eyes downward
is a window shade,
damask, steely against the sun.

Coyote City

Every year more

cuts through new
ground. Buildup

creeps the entirety.
I sit on our patio

at what used to be
city edge, hear
the cry of your wood saw

mix with the aftersound
of bitterness.
It's what you do.

All roads lead—
those built and those
not yet.

This city eats stars
scattered across sky darkness
by howling dogs, eats

the heat of virgin terrain,
churns it into valence
clumping desert homes,

eats the bones.
Bigger. Better.

Built and not yet planned.
You and I, a blueprint

for lost causes,
measures taken,

tumbleweed left.
All roads lead in.

Straight in
I once went. Now

turn at the end.

4. Dying Room—
For the Gone, the Diminished

'Twas comfort in her Dying Room
To hear the living Clock—

—Emily Dickinson

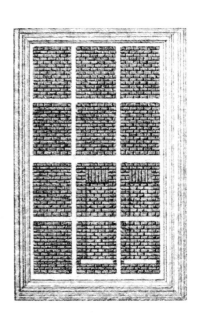

Springing Abbie Hoffman from Jail

My friend and I are teaching night college sociology
in the early 80s when she gets the idea that since
the only way to support a revolution is to make your own,
we should invite Abbie Hoffman to meet our students
because he's got a jail sentence that allows him
to get out to talk in schools, as long as he returns at night,
so we figure that we'll have time for a little fun too
before curfew because we hate the thought of his sitting in jail
staring at the inside of his head, just because of a little cocaine.
When he shows up, our students are subdued,
don't know who he is, never heard of the dollar bills
tossed onto the floor of the New York Stock Exchange,
look confused about that because isn't the point
to *make* money not toss it away and maybe he can give
advice on how to become a celebrity. We can see
this isn't going over well and decide to end class early
and take him for drinks with dinner at The Ginger Man,
named for Donleavy's character also on the edge of madness,
but Abbie's so sad and we think he doesn't like us,
though really it's that he's on the depressed end of bipolar
(years before he swallows 150 phenobarbital pills) and can't stop
talking about how dull jail is, to which I reply
it's not as much fun is it, as fifty thousand people
trying to levitate the Pentagon, which finally gets a smile
as he says, hey—but didn't you see it rise?

Ephemera

He says that in the dark we feel the same
—his dead wife and me; cleft to me,

I think he means not the waxed weight
and heft of her, but the whispery

memory. I imagine
the razor-cut vein, the schism of skin,

one hundred Seconals swallowed,
scattered on the perfect terra cotta floor with her.

Or maybe it happened a different way.
I cannot ask.

From the closet's cedar boxiness, I try on her soft
black napa jacket to see if

what he says is true, that we
are sized like twins. A second skin, a suffocation

of the one beneath—the fit, a body bag.
It will be years before I can afford to buy myself

a jacket like this. When he too
will be susurrus, ghost of a synapse, grist.

Mr. Verner asks New York not to spoil his friend, the Bushman

—New York Daily Tribune, *Oct. 3, 1906*

When Ota Benga is locked in the primate house
with a parrot and an orangutan at the Bronx Zoo,
sunlight hurts. For too long, he was in
the darkness of the Museum of Natural History,
for too long, he was displayed at the St. Louis Fair.
He's too long away from both his dead wives.
The Kasai River, its tangled edge of rubber,
palm, teak, is not real in this forest of cages—harsh
clang and leering laughter from spectral faces
looking at him. The ghost people don't believe
he has desires, this pygmy *Missing Link*.
He wants his home. His house was burned.
No Congo village exists anymore, no clan.
Just yelling, poking, clinging—
the clamor to see his filed, pointed teeth.

The ghost-man Verner had bought him from the king
for five American dollars after wine, food,
drums for an honored visitor.
Transport in a hammock was not for Ota Benga.
He'd gone to hunt an elephant. Came back to this.

Exhibited each afternoon during September,
says a sign on his cage. At first, they let him out
to walk the zoo in a white suit,
though they laugh and burn him with cigarettes.
Yesterday, the police were called—
they've taken away his knife.
The Edison machine, belonging to the ghost men,
steals the soul from his body.
He listens to it on a cylinder; the voice says,
you'll never get a steamship back to Africa,
get a gun, aim backward toward your heart.

Omega

On Far Rockaway Beach, I found a horseshoe crab.
I was young and it was dead,
intact in its carapace as if it had just stepped
sadly from the sea, its spidery legs

no longer able to regenerate.
Spring—the tides wash treasure onto land.
I shivered in the wind.

The sky was gray, the way I like the ocean—
harsh, but color-muted on the shell-flecked sand.
I took it home. Dried,
tied in a plastic bag, forgotten.

Sifting through storage, cleaning out
my parents' house after their deaths, I find
the picked-clean useless armor,
shell of the horseshoe crab. Nothing left between,
within, neither maggots, stink, nor remnant carcass.

And then what didn't change—we couldn't shelve
our shelled-in selves.
Nor could I keep much more than this.

Interior

—after Bonnard

You slip into my dream grumpy with loss. Again,
I explain why I no longer go to Taormina,

why I moved out of your bedroom, its walls
painted red last winter. I've missed you,

your half-closed door. Your tongue, devil lips.
Your hands, how they bracketed my body. You were

a major racketeering enterprise, promised fire,
opals on my soles. I refused to be the mistress,

to kill myself when confronted by the wife.
I refused to be a Marthe, breaking

apart into the furnishings. How dare you paint me
into the picture only after she died! The what-might-

have-been, I could have turned around, torn
at your kidney. I could have stayed there, watched

you bleed. What would it taste like to chew
your bones for dinner? My teeth are not what

they used to be. Worn talons too. Hell—I could cry
at the moon-mirror with your visage, but I won't.

After the Last Inca Ruler

These people are us from a few hundred years ago.
             —Puruchuco Site Project Leader,
                         Tupac Amaru

Swath of cloth   feathers and seeds
bundles of mummy
forgotten centuries under the earth
of a hillside ravine
streaked with rot from seeping
sewage from shantytown
streets where no rain may fall
for twenty years.
Their eyes are still there

stare out at Pizarro
mistaken for the son of Viracocha
the white-skinned god
whose cannon controlled thunder
stare at the ghost of Atahualpa
—at steel and cavalry
armies of smallpox   measles   influenza
famine   Francisco de Toledo
and all that came after.

Every variety of dead—perfect
to predict elections,
notes an archaeologist,
as if they would feel the warmth
of the immortal sun and rise to vote.
Hidden fetal-positioned with pots
animal skins   corn—a baby.
Falsas cabezas—false heads
for the wealthy
wigged and filled with cotton.
No one knows why.
Ancient graves
barely nuzzled in the earth
of a dust-ridden schoolyard.

Squatters have fled here from highland guerillas—
afraid of the living
afraid of the dead.
If they find a mummy they burn it with gasoline.

It is their story.
It is not their story.

Apartment House, New York City, 1 A.M.

On the high terrace,
in a white silk robe,
she counts stars, extrapolates
what's made invisible by ambient light.
They don't answer her calls,
coy celestials
heavy with solitude.
Next to the boxed geraniums,

the iron rail is bolted into place.
It, too, knows the cumberment.

One floor above,
the little black dog howls
—sharing disquiet,
a lament for the Lamb in America.

The woman on the terrace,
her despair is hard
as the waves of her hair—she wants
to feel the flight.
There's tightness in her grip.
She understands too well
the astonishment, the brevity
of birds.

Sanjûrô, as Played by Toshirô Mifune, Occupies the Body of a Yard Guy

Kurosawa underscores Sanjûrô's identity as a vestigial, marginal figure, useful or even essential in crisis situations, but...destined to disappear in the end.
—*J Kohn*, Literature Film Quarterly

In real life, he's smaller than on film,
divorced from camera angles, prop sword,
no strut walk as he pushes his cart—
rōnin without kimono.
It takes getting used to, a bent body.
He's home—home from myth,
from the wrangle, from the coffin-maker
busily banging wood together,
from a thousand years of conflict
worn like pool shorts.

On this Oahu of subsonic Tomahawks,
modern warriors, traffic jams, and heat,
he makes his daily landscape rounds,
makes methodical turns on the sprinkler valve,
every one a different responsive sigh.
Sometimes, an orchid or anthurium
needs tending and will sing to him.

A woman wrapped in a towel comes to the door
just as he takes a break. In her garage,
he unpacks his *ono*, his rice.
His quiet time, he drifts,
remembers the sweet moment he took away
a gangster's pistol.
He likes to look at her, this woman in a towel.
These are the things that still
belong to him, that return to him.

Talk About Consciousness

You lie on your side in this bathroom,
lavender aromatherapy soaps and white towels,
surprised at ending up *here*—on marble tiles.

Be Here Now, said Ram Dass, transformation
notwithstanding. Your mind wanders—India
—Taj Mahal—light shifting color,
white marble.

Eat here now, says the corner coffee shop.
You noticed it yesterday—not thinking
about head injury as a lifestyle.
Like hamburger meat, brain cells
slough off in some kind of cognitive dandruff.

In here, the alarm ringing in your ears suggests
a quick exit—but to where is not clear; this might
be just a practice drill.
Can you continue to lie here, to be here?
Asana, Pranayama,
where's my mantra—damn it—

you're somewhere cool and then—a freefall
into a different theology; you liked
the lightheadedness of lysergic acid
so much better than this. Forget about it—
only the present matters; as George Harrison sang,
Why try to live a life that isn't real?

Weeping,
you're scared of betrayal—of no longer being
here, not vital matter but a smatter of dust.

Your mind out somewhere—a teenager
with multiple piercings and nowhere to return
but the Sears-anchored
mall of your middle-aged body which now
sits up, blots
the blood on the bridge of your purpling nose.

A Diagonal Break

along the foot abuses the socket.
Later, like a child's drawing
clipped to a light-box,
I'm shown one side of the Matterhorn
imaged in x-ray grays.
A bleached room.
Bones

are the first to go.
So this is the beginning
of what can be expected: swim
accidents and leaching
of vigor from the basilisk. Loss—
a subject hardly slighted by muses' wind.
My bassoon of a body, splintered
at one edge by beached rock
—mournful to be ruining in sand.

As If the Sand Were Stone

Stones clumped everywhere,
a rocky shore,
I step barefoot, feel the pain, grimace. Sharp,
before the cold shock of early-May
Ligurian salt—depths
lumber into lechery
from winter, if it's winter in the water.

What do I really know of thick murk,
its braille and swoosh? A bully wave breaks
bulky around me, shrinks me into myself.
I want to be diminished in my bikini too small
for the bearings of my history.
I could walk away from here, or deeper
into the unknown, moon and gravity, not yet
evening with its dark.
Water, verge—I'm illiterate as to options.

I am a woman with options, I reassure
myself as I make smaller moves in the surf
to avoid new distress on the instep, seductive
potential wound. In this deserted water,
everything's numbered.

Yesterday, in the hills above town
following ridge markers I thought I knew,
I found myself on a gravel ledge,
staring at that abyss. The old refrain,
though the sunlight, with the distant sea
flickering, was a tricky light switch.

Incantation

The best thing to die from is living.
Let me kill myself slowly with pleasure.

Let me dance round and round in circles first.
Let me blow a lot of fuses.

Let me age like a good slab of steak, tender
with the mold trimmed. Let me be

a car going 80 miles per hour.
Let me reach 80—the exquisite

torture of those many years is compelling.
Let them not be Chaplinesque. Let them say

she never knew what hit her. Let it be like
the one James Dean got, only much later.

Let me not surrender to humiliations.
Let me end when my mind, still sharp,

is somewhere else—dreaming of perfectly
grilled lamb, the rosemary perfume so strong,

it could be sealed in my pillow, of hot sex,
and let that be not so long gone

that it burns like a bad joke. In the valley
of the shadow of death, I'd still like

my red lipstick please. Let my breasts not reach
my waist. Let there be very little

scar tissue on me at the time and
let there be a weeping willow, under it

a significantly younger man,
my own little honey cake, who is weeping,

too—though I don't wish that on him for long.
He'll have a life to live.

Special Thanks

With special thanks to Eric Hoffmann for contributing the inside drawing, to Margo Taft Stever for her incisive commentary on an earlier draft of *4 Rms w Vu* and much appreciation also to Larry W. Moore for feedback on some of the poems and to Mervyn Taylor, Elizabeth Haukaas, Myra Malkin, Lynn McGee, and Larry Loeb also, for their unselfish poetic insights and friendships.

About the Author

Susana H. Case is a Professor and Program Coordinator at the New York Institute of Technology. Her photos have appeared in *Blue Hour Magazine, pacificREVIEW*, and *San Pedro River Review*, among others. Author of several chapbooks, her Slapering Hol Press chapbook, *The Scottish Café*, was published in a dual-language version, *Kawiarnia Szkocka*, by Poland's Opole University Press. Her previous books of poetry are: *Salem In Séance* (WordTech Editions), *Elvis Presley's Hips & Mick Jagger's Lips* (Anaphora Literary Press), and *Earth and Below* (Anaphora Literary Press). Please visit her online at: http://iris.nyit.edu/~shcase/.

Other Recent Titles from Mayapple Press:

Marjorie Stelmach, *Without Angels,* 2014
    Paper, 74pp, $15.95 plus s&h
    ISBN 978-1-936419-37-1
David Lunde, *The Grandson of Heinrich Schliemann & Other Truths and Fictions,* 2014
    Paper, 62pp, $14.95 plus s&h
    ISBN 978-1-936419-36-4
Eleanor Lerman, *Strange Life,* 2014
    Paper, 90pp, $15.95 plus s&h
    ISBN 978-1-936419-35-7
Sally Rosen Kindred, *Book of Asters,* 2014
    Paper, 74pp, $15.95 plus s&h
    ISBN 978-1-936419-34-0
Gretchen Primack, *Doris' Red Spaces,* 2014
    Paper, 74pp, $15.95 plus s&h
    ISBN 978-1-936419-33-3
Stephen Lewandowski, *Under Foot,* 2014
    Paper, 80pp, $15.95 plus s&h
    ISBN 978-1-936419-32-6
Hilma Contreras (Judith Kerman, Tr.), *Between Two Silences/ Entre Dos Silencios,* 2013
    Paper, 126pp, $16.95 plus s&h
    ISBN 978-1-936419-31-9
Helen Ruggieri & Linda Underhill, Eds., *Written on Water: Writings about the Allegheny River,* 2013
    Paper, 108pp, $19.95 plus s&h (includes Bonus CD)
    ISBN 978-1-936419-30-2
Don Cellini, *Candidates for sainthood and other sinners/ Aprendices de santo y otros pecadores,* 2013
    Paper, 62pp, $14.95 plus s&h
    ISBN 978-1-936419-29-6
Gerry LaFemina, *Notes for the Novice Ventriloquist,* 2013
    Paper, 78pp, $15.95 plus s&h
    ISBN 978-1-936419-28-9
Robert Haight, *Feeding Wild Birds,* 2013
    Paper, 82pp, $15.95 plus s&h
    ISBN 978-1-936419-27-2
Pamela Miller, *Miss Unthinkable,* 2013
    Paper, 58pp, $14.95 plus s&h
    ISBN 978-1-936419-26-5

For a complete catalog of Mayapple Press publications, please visit our website at *www.mayapplepress.com*. Books can be ordered direct from our website with secure on-line payment using PayPal, or by mail (check or money order). Or order through your local bookseller.